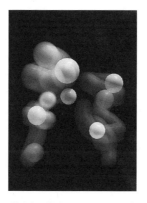

"Kick a living system, and
you can expect the unexpected"
DAVID FRIED

Philosophical Thinking is Yoga for the Mind®

Fatal W H Y
Numbers
C
O
U
N
T

O
HANS MAGNUS N
ENZENSBERGER

TRANSLATED FROM THE GERMAN BY KAREN LEEDER

C
H
WITH A FOREWORD BY A
GERD GIGERENZER N
C
E

UPPER WEST SIDE PHILOSOPHERS, INC. • NEW YORK • 2011

Published by Upper West Side Philosophers, Inc. / P. O. Box 250645, New York, NY
10025, USA / www.westside-philosophers.com

Yoga for the Mind®

Shorter versions of the essays in this book were first delivered as public lectures:
"Fatal Numbers" at the Festival della Matematica in Rome, Italy, on March 13, 2008;
"On the Metaphysical Antics of Mathematics" at the University Club, Bonn, Germany
(under the auspices of the Max Planck Institute for
Mathematics), on October 22, 2008.

Our special thanks to Paul Newman for reviewing the manuscript, and to David Fried
for allowing us to use his "Way of Words, No.1, 2008" as a cover image, and for creating additional original artwork in response to Hans Magnus Enzensberger's text on
p.6 ("A-WOW-HME"), p.10 ("B-WOW-HME"), p.36 ("F-WOW-HME"), and p.50 ("D-
WOW-HME"). All images copyright © 2010 by David Fried

Library of Congress Cataloging-in-Publication Data

Enzensberger, Hans Magnus.
[Fortuna und Kalkül. English]
Fatal numbers : why count on chance / Hans Magnus Enzensberger ; translated from
the German by Karen Leeder ; with a foreword by Gerd Gigerenzer.
    p. cm. -- (Subway line ; no. 3)
Includes bibliographical references (p.   ).
ISBN 978-1-935830-01-6 (pbk. : alk. paper)
1. Probabilities--Philosophy. 2. Chance. I. Title.
QA273.A35E5913 2011
519.2--dc22

                    2010043287

Typesetting and Design: Michael Eskin
Printed by Offset Impressions, Inc., Reading, PA
Printed in the United States of America

ACC LIBRARY SERVICES AUSTIN, TX

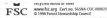

CONTENTS

Foreword / 7

*

FATAL NUMBERS / 11

ON THE METAPHYSICAL ANTICS OF
MATHEMATICS / 37

*

Select Bibliography / 51

Contributors / 52

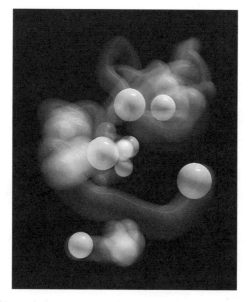

"From that moment on, there was to be no more talk
of fate but instead of its atrophied cousin: chance."
H. M. ENZENSBERGER

FOREWORD

Two gorgeously dressed young women sit upright on two chairs calmly facing each other, yet neither is aware of the other's beauty. One is blindfolded, a wheel in her left hand, which human figures desperately climb, cling to, or tumble from; the other gazes into a hand-mirror, lost in admiration of herself. The blindfolded beauty is Fortuna—the fickle, wheel-toting goddess of chance. Her companion is sober Sapientia—the calculating, vain, divine being of science. The portrait was made in Paris some 500 years ago.

Hans Magnus Enzensberger's book is about the breakdown of the opposition between Fortuna and Sapientia's alter ego, science. It is about the golden fruits of their intimate relationship, and the attempts of each to snatch the other's possessions. Science sought to liberate humans from Fortuna's wheel, to banish luck, and replace chances with causes. Fortuna struck back by undermining science itself with chance and creating the vast empire of probability and statistics. After their struggles neither remained the same: Fortuna was tamed, and science lost its certainty.

Today, we live in the mesmerizing world created by these two allegorical figures. Our minds have become crowded with numbers, with probabilities of earthquakes, rain, and everything else. Baseball grew out of sandlots and city streets, supported by a culture of working men and farm boys. Now it is unthinkable without statistics: batting averages, strikeout averages, and playing the percentages. If forced to choose, many a fan would rather see the numbers than the game. Markets and trading were brought about by daring, worldly-wise men who traveled across empires and made their fortunes, surpassing the ruling aristocracy in wealth and eventually initiating a revolution so that others without titles of nobility could live a decent life. Today, financial markets define trading, traders like to bet rather than travel, and mathematical models aim at predicting the stock market. Meanwhile, blindfolded Fortuna continues plying *her* trade, calmly spinning her wheel and plunging Nobel laureates' high-leverage hedge funds into ruin …

We call on governments for more bureaucracy and regulation, but rarely for education on how to live with uncertainty. H. G. Wells once said that if we want efficient citizenship in a modern technological society, we need to teach everyone three things: reading, writing, and the language of statistics and probability. In Western countries, we have taught almost everyone reading and writing, but not how to reckon with risks and handle uncertainties. Our children are taught the mathematics of certainty—geometry and trigonometry—but not the mathematics of uncertainty they need for life after school. High-tech *Homo sapiens* remains an alien in the world created by the two beauties, awkwardly stuttering rather than fluently speaking the new language of probability. The weather report announces a 30% chance of rain tomorrow—30% of what? In a study I conducted, most citizens in Amsterdam and Berlin believed that this means that it will rain tomorrow 30% of the time, that is, for seven or eight hours. Others thought it means that it will rain in 30% of the area. Most New Yorkers thought it means rain on 30% of the days for which the prediction is made.

Not understanding the new language is one thing. Being falsely impressed by new technologies that promise to tame chance is another. Every year we support a $200 billion industry that calculates future predictions, mostly erroneous, from market tips to exchange rates to population explosions. The conviction that predictions automatically improve by designing more sophisticated computers and buying terabytes of information is a fantasy. Blind trust in calculation has become a modern form of superstition nourished by scores of clever fortune sellers. And the illusory certainty of numbers has become a threat to the survival of sound judgment: the genuine human capacity for good intuition.

Opening Hans Magnus Enzensberger's book, we look into a mirror. It makes us reflect. In the reflection we begin to see our own hopes, fears, and desire for knowledge. We are enjoined to confront our illusions of certainty, marvel at the dazzling unpredictability of the future, and enter into the beautiful world of ideas that Fortuna and Sapientia have opened to us.

GERD GIGERENZER

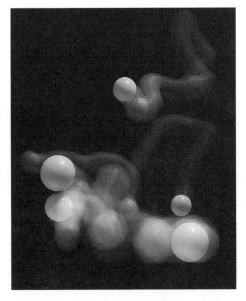

"Besides, people behave rather differently from dice. They are, for example, capable of lying."
H. M. ENZENSBERGER

FATAL NUMBERS

> The fairest cosmos is but a pile of sweepings thrown down at random.
>
> HERACLITUS

I

Always this uncertainty! Only the dead no longer take any risks. For all of human history, people have invented methods for coming to terms with the seemingly unpredictable vicissitudes of existence. No early society managed without shamans, soothsayers, magicians, astrologers, or priests. Oracles, amulets, and incantations belonged to the indispensable techniques for interpreting and influencing the fate of communities and individuals alike. And it's certainly no secret that all these methods still enjoy great popularity today.

When it came to the old gods, one had to follow the Greek goddess Tyche, or Fortuna for the Romans, in order to catch hold of one's little bit of good fortune. These capricious gods were not in the business of bringing eternal bliss, but they were responsible for the random opportunities that our existence on earth gives or withholds. The important thing was to choose the right moment. This relationship to time was embodied by one particular little god or daemon: Caerus. In mythology, he is known as the youngest son of Zeus. He is easily recognized by the way his hair is depicted; any attempt to grasp him from behind is in vain, the back of his head being bald. One must grasp him before he passes, by the tuft of hair hanging over his forehead, in order to seize the opportune moment.

Of course, modernity was not satisfied with these ancient methods handed down over generations. On the contrary, scientific thinking was determined to make a decisive break with what it deemed to be superstition. In the place of superstition there was to be calculation—a project aiming at nothing less than the rationalization of fortune. From that moment on, there was to be no more talk of fate but instead of its atrophied cousin: chance.

II

At the forefront of this offensive were the mathematicians. In 1524, Girolamo Cardano published *On Casting the Die*. This treatise on dice games marks the beginning of the history of probability theory. The Renaissance scholar from Padua was a passionate gambler. Alongside mathematical calculations, the book also contained all kinds of advice for tricksters and con artists, and Cardano himself was rumored to have had a hand in all kinds of dubious practices, not to say outright swindling.

Subsequent champions of probability calculation like Pierre de Fermat and Jacob Bernoulli were also fascinated by the game of chance. Pascal even went as far as imagining belief in God as a kind of game that involved simply deciding heads or tails. He claimed that it was more rational to plump for the existence of God: If you bet on that and win, you win everything; whereas if you lose, you lose nothing. Quite apart from the fact that a calculation along those lines doesn't really hold up to scrutiny on logical grounds, and might moreover seem strange or perverse, it was certainly meant in earnest. Nothing would have been further from the mind of a believer and Jansenist like Pascal than a frivolous reckoning with religious questions.

(Even the gods on Olympus were addicted to dice. The three brothers Zeus, Poseidon, and Hades are supposed to have divided the world between them on the throw of the dice; the heavens fell to Zeus, the oceans to Poseidon, and the underworld to Hades. The word 'calculation', by the way, derives from the Latin 'calculus', which means something like 'little stone'. Originally, small black-and-white stones served as oracles, talismans, and mementos of happy or unhappy events. Later, they were used as a means of casting votes to condemn or acquit the accused, and only at the end of their career did they end up on the gaming board.)

III

It seems that classical theory has succeeded in calculating probabilities in games of dice throwing and coin tossing down to the last decimal point. Of course, this not only presupposes the existence of ideal coins and dice such as do not actually exist in the real world, but the calculation also depends on the law of large numbers that Bernoulli discovered towards the end of the 17th century. Only if the experiment is repeated an infinite number of times is the average value as expected. Unfortunately, no one has a limitless time to spend at the gaming tables. For one thing, human life is too short.

Besides, even simple questions like "Heads or tails?" or "Red or black?" are enough of a challenge for common sense. You are playing roulette, and the ball lands on red twenty or thirty times running. Don't you believe that a sequence like this strains the bounds of probability? Aren't you already itching to bet on black because you imagine the chances of black increasing with every subsequent roll? Wrong! Each new roll of the ball is completely unaffected by all the ones that have gone before. Indeed, things look even worse for you. According to the law of large numbers, the ratio between the number of red and black results approaches 50:50 the longer the game is played. But the actual results can deviate markedly. For this reason (and others like it), the multitude of systems that gamblers develop in the hope of getting ahead are doomed to failure. You often see cast-iron propositions on the internet. It's rather like the famous advert that promises a surefire way of getting rich quick if you send in five dollars. The secret formula that is finally revealed is: "Do what I've done." There's only one thing that's certain in gambling: in the end the bank always wins. (The lottery only pays out about 50% of the receipts. The other half goes to the organization behind it.)

So, if you choose to trust your instincts, in the long term you're lost, as the entertaining game of birthday guessing shows. Suppose you had invited 23 people to a party. With the hosts there would be 25 people present in total. What do you reckon are the chances that two of you actually have the same birthday? Because the year has 365 days you might perhaps think: "Right, I'll divide 365 by two; then there would have to be 183 present in order for there to be a 50:50 chance that at least two of the guests might be celebrating their birthday on the same day." Hopefully, there are no mathematicians among you, for a mathematician would immediately shout out: "Wrong! The probability of that occurring is pretty exactly 50.7%."

Surprises like this are a little less entertaining when it's a question of life and death—as in treatments for cancer for example. Supposing you are a member of a population group in which every hundredth person sooner or later succumbs to a cancer-related illness. This is a far from pleasant prospect, and so you perhaps decide to do one of those tests that health insurance companies recommend in the name of taking proper precautions. Not that any of these tests is infallible. Furthermore, let's assume that the procedure used by the doctor has been proved to be reliable in 79% of cases. This means naturally that 21% of the patients will endure a false alarm. If the specialist informs you that your test result is positive, which in medical terms of course means negative, you will doubtless suffer several sleepless nights. But what's the probability that you really have cancer? Not only you but also the majority of doctors will overestimate the risk—perhaps you will even reckon it at 79%. In reality, it's just 3.6%! "Well," the mathematician will tell you, "that's what comes of not knowing Bayes' theorem." It's a shock, of course. But one begins to see the kind of paradoxes and complexities that lie ahead when one gets involved with the calculation of probability.

IV

The basic principle, meanwhile, sounds quite straightforward. In the words of Pierre Simon de Laplace's *Analytical Theory of Probability* (1812): "The probability of a particular event is calculated by the number of ways that this event can occur divided by the number of ways that all possible events can occur—as long as they are all equally probable as in a game of dice."

However, that's not usually the case; and certain events happen more frequently than others. Even this though can be calculated if enough data is available. In his book *The Doctrine of Chances* (1733), Abraham de Moivre, a French émigré who had fled to England and became friends with Isaac Newton, showed how this works (Carl Friedrich Gauß is often falsely credited with this discovery). He offered the first statement of the formula for the so-called 'normal distribution curve', a symmetrical function in which the values of the random variable cluster around the mean and become more seldom as they move further away from it. If one plots the results on a Cartesian coordinate system it comes out every time as the famous bell curve that is so seductively and immediately persuasive:

Probability density functions of the normal distribution of random variables with different parameter values.

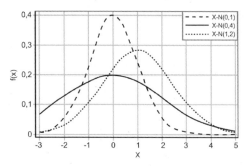

This applies not only to dice games but to all possible measurable values that can be calculated statistically, regardless of whether one is dealing with life expectancy, observational errors, Brownian motion, the modeling of damage data for insurance companies, or the calculation of annuities. For example, if one measures as large a sample of people as possible, it can quickly be seen that there are relatively few giants or dwarves. The curve reaches its peak at the mean, which is important to know if one happens to be a manufacturer of shoes. It wouldn't be advisable to make an equal number of shoes in all sizes from 6 to 14; if one did, one would be left with a large number of items one simply couldn't shift.

V

In this way, many economic, technical, and physical phenomena can be described, if not quite precisely, then at least fairly approximately. Unfortunately, there's a catch, which is not simply a matter of chance, for whenever one is dealing with probabilities there's always a catch. Thus, it's not quite clear how big the sample must be if the result is to be even halfway useful. How many feet the shoe manufacturer has to measure to make sure that his supply meets demand is a question that has had statisticians wracking their brains for years, and their answers still leave something to be desired.

The theoretical value of the integral of the bell curve can never reach 100% since the curve only meets the abscissae in infinity (to the left and right of the maximum). "That's not important," the statistician will say, "since giants measuring 8 feet are so extremely unlikely that they can be ignored." Things are rather different in the case of a detective who wants to convict a suspect on the basis of a DNA test. The probability of an error occurring is reckoned to be tiny. Molecular geneticists insist that the chances are one in a billion. "Not an issue," the judge will say, and sentence the accused without a qualm.

Identical or non-identical DNA, a shoe size of 6 or 14, cancer or no cancer—these are at least questions that allow for an unambiguous answer. The softer the data, the less compelling the conclusions that can be drawn. A glance at standard intelligence testing is enough to make this clear. With their beloved intelligence quotient, the devisors of IQ tests only measure what they themselves conceive of as intelligence. The closer someone comes to their ideal self-image, the better the results. In this way, the researchers can deliver their perfect bell curve, but they regularly fail when it comes to the cognitive faculties of people who don't fit their mold. The results produced by Amazonian Indians, schizophrenics, or wonderfully inventive actors serve only to undermine the experiments because they deliver proof of the simple fact that intelligence cannot be measured. Market researchers and opinion pollsters are even less discriminating. They are the rumormongers of statistics, whose job it is to keep an ear out wherever they go and repeat everything they hear. While some of them are interested in which toothpaste the majority prefers, others want to know the dominant mood of the public, which politicians voters most despise, or which prejudices they cling to most fervently. In the course of their researches, these harmless spies don't usually bother with nine-digit numbers. In fact, they make do with surprisingly small samples, typically relying on 1000–2000 'randomly' chosen subjects who are deemed 'representative'.

Clearly, the answers also depend on the kinds of questions put, and the results are often further modified according to some arcane criteria before reaching the public. Among professionals, this is called 'massaging the data'. Besides, people behave rather differently from dice. They are, for example, capable of lying. Not that today's researchers, who have learned from bitter experience, any longer share the same blithe naïveté as Alfred Kinsey, who famously believed everything his subjects chose to report about their sexual habits. That's why they try to catch their subjects out with control questions. In this game of cat and mouse everything naturally depends on who is the shrewdest player: the underpaid company employee trudging door to door or on the end of a phone, or the supposed representative of the general public who, it is assumed (and not always correctly), will not see through the trick questions.

A similar battle of wills takes place whenever experienced candidates set out to measure themselves against examining institutions of one kind or another. Before any exam or interview, they analyze all the practices, criteria, and even the whims of their opposite number in microscopic detail and formulate their answers accordingly. In this way, they undertake to examine their examiner, which, it goes without saying, can diminish the reliability of the results in no small measure. The mania for Progress in International Student Assessment (PISA) in higher education offers some of the best examples.

VI

If you find all these mathematical highways and byways exhausting, it might be time for a short break so that you can relax before things begin to get worse; and unfortunately, anyone who invokes chance must always count on things getting worse. For this fleeting force, which is so valuable to statisticians because it bestows on them the aura of neutrality and objectivity, cannot be formalized in any exact way.

"But this can't be so very difficult," you will say, "in the world I live in there are literally thousands of random occurrences every day, all I need to do is to write them down as they happen." And that's exactly how the first lists of random numbers came into being, and of course the people who compiled them once again turned to their old favorite: the game of chance. They simply wrote down the results of as many roulette games as possible in the hope of thus arriving at an absolutely structureless series of numbers. Unfortunately, there's no such thing as an *ideal* game of roulette because there are no ideal machines and no ideal croupiers. At best, the results might offer a reasonable ap-

proximation, not being based on an *ideal* random generator. "No problem," you might object, "my computer can do
that, with the push of a button it can generate as many random numbers as you wish."

Your confidence does you credit, and it may well be that
the programmers you put your faith in do indeed have the
best of intentions. Nevertheless, any experienced player
knows how easily one is tempted to cheat a little here and
there. The fact is that your generator can only deliver results that are *a bit* random. But what on earth can this possibly mean: a bit? It smacks rather of the unfortunate out-
come: 'a bit pregnant'. If you don't find this satisfactory,
then you will have to take recourse to the oldest gambling
maxim in the book: *Corriger la fortune!* And that's exactly
how your computer does it, too: it performs a little sleight
of hand without you noticing. The numbers as they appear
are all generated by a fully deterministic program so that in
principle nothing about them is unpredictable. A semblance
of chance is being simulated for you. "At least, that's better
than nothing," you might well say. It's certainly enough to
fill in a lottery ticket.

Mathematicians, on the other hand, might not be so dif-
fident. But even they know that there's nothing better to
be had. A computer, no matter how powerful, can only generate random sequences that are less complex than its program. As a result, the machine simply cannot decide whether a particular list of numbers is genuinely random or not, as
Gregory Chaitin demonstrated more than half a century
ago. And what's worse, he proved that there are countless
mathematical statements that are essentially uncomput-
able. Whether they are true or false is precisely a matter of
chance. Chaitin's theorem has certain subterranean links
with Kurt Gödel's incompleteness theorem and Alan Tur-

ing's theses on the 'decision problem'; and you can bet your bottom dollar that that's *not* a matter of chance.

VII

Modern probability theory has not allowed itself to be blown off course by such devastating conclusions. Its leading lights have no notion of throwing in the towel. Admirable persistence! Even though only the most seasoned experts can follow all the subtleties that are being juggled here. People like us must bow before Andrey Nikolaevich Kolmogorov's axioms of probability, just as we must capitulate before the Chernoff inequality, which keeps probability theorists entertained. Another of science's great achievements can, however, be sketched in just a few words, at least in outline. I mean the so-called Monte Carlo method, whose very name bespeaks the fixed idea of probability theorists that the world resembles a casino. Certainly, this partiality to gambling can be looked on with a degree of indulgence. Much more ominous was the event that led to the method's development. As so often in science, weapons technology proved to be the mother of progress. In the 1940s and 1950s, the elite of American physics had assembled in the New Mexican desert to advance with the Manhattan project. At the beginning of the 1950s, the first hydrogen bomb was developed in Los Alamos. At this point, it was discovered that the experts were not in a position to calculate the diffusion of neutrons in the fissile material with any precision. Two émigrés from Eastern Europe, Stanislaw Ulam and John von Neumann, hit upon the idea of simulating many thousands of random solutions for the problem and saving the best ones in each case. Without the help of the first electronic computers, in the development of which both men had been pivotal, this wouldn't have been possible. Unfortunately though, the Monte Carlo method also has one small flaw: Its results can be wrong. Admittedly, the probability of error can be ever further reduced by frequent repetition of the algorithm, but it never reaches zero. In other words, an experiment as risky as the detonation of the first hydrogen bomb could also have gone badly wrong. Its inventors were entirely aware of this fact and simply took the risk into account.

At the level of computer technology that exists today it is possible to generate millions of test runs per second, thus significantly reducing the quota of errors. That's why the Monte Carlo method is routinely used in order to find at least approximate numerical answers to complex mathematical problems that can either not be solved through analytical calculations at all, or would require a computational effort beyond our power. The reason is that we are dealing here with stochastic processes based on a large number of nonlinear conditions. That's the case, for instance, in transport planning, production optimization, climate research, queue-length calculation, business administration, and mathematical finance. The experts seek to comfort themselves and others about the fact that only approximate solutions are possible by insisting on how small the probability is that what they have come up with might be wrong. They typically say, "It's 98% certain that the value lies somewhere between 0.75 and 0.77," and then add that at least this statement is "100% true." Whether this is enough to reassure someone involved in high-risk ventures is, needless to say, doubtful.

VIII

Obvious pitfalls await anyone who gets too cozy with the much-maligned sister of probability theory: statistics. These two could be compared with the two Annas from *The Seven Deadly Sins of the Petty Bourgeoisie* (a ballet chanté by Kurt Weill and Bertolt Brecht). "My sister is beautiful," the first Anna sings, "but I am practical." Not quite unjustly it is said of statistics, this all too willing accomplice, that it entertains a certain complicity with untruth. And it's not so much potty-trained mathematical theory that is to blame but messy reality itself. As Ian Stewart has noted, "statistics is remarkable for the way its ideas ebb and flow between the physical and social sciences." It began by analyzing observational errors for instance in astronomy, and applied the methods it developed there to social phenomena. One of the pioneers of the discipline was Sir Francis Galton. He is not only responsible for the theory of regression, but we also have him to thank for inventing the notion of eugenics. He even proposed breeding an intellectually and morally superior race based on it.

Some of the other temptations of statistics appear rather more benign. Going back to the raw data with which it operates, let's take the calculation of the gross domestic product as an example. The GDP includes the sum total of all fixing, maintenance, and 'therapy' costs in any given society, which means that with every accident, illness, and crime this marvelous indicator rises, naturally causing the public to wax optimistic. For political reasons, unemployment is measured differently in each country, though as a rule always with a good deal of cunning. According to a declaration of the European Commission, you are classified as poor if you earn less than half of the average income. This means that poverty has been assured a form of eternal existence; for even if the annual per capita income were to rise to two million, by this definition those with only one million would sink into poverty. Conversely, a growth rate of 200% sounds impressive, but it doesn't do anything for the person who will now starve on three dollars a month instead of one.

Admittedly, this can lead to very crude errors. And what does 'average' really mean? Does it refer to the arithmetic mean, the median, or the modal value? As long as something as basic as that isn't clear, one could conclude from a statistical calculation that the water supply is functioning perfectly if one half of the population is drowning while the other half is dying of thirst.

Such simple misinterpretations can of course only befall the gullible general public. The experienced statistician is made of sterner stuff. And where it's a question of big bucks, as in the insurance business for instance, the calculation of probability has proved its worth many times over. Here, too, as in the casino, the motto that the bank always wins rules the day. Bernoulli's law of large numbers sees to it. The more customers in the insurer's portfolio, the less the insurer has to fear from loss. Where the risks accumulate, or are particularly high, they are spread by means of reinsurance onto broader shoulders. The calculation works precisely because the pool of insurers doesn't care if the house of the insured burns down, or if he dies. In actuarial mathematics, just as "in stochastics or in the discussions of chance in game theory," one seldom encounters, as Odo Marquard has emphasized, "the perspective of the person who is served up with the results of creation or of other accidents of fate."

IX

Calculations concerning future events, unlike statistical analyses of distributions in the present, are not empirically verifiable data but bets. As soon as the prognostic potential of probability theory is called upon, a whole new dimension comes into play that poses far more fundamental questions than any discussion about observational error. Where research into future probability cannot rely on available data uncertainty is rife. Whether it is dealing with economic trends, long-range weather forecasts, or market speculation, the results are—and there's no other way to put it—devastating. Hardly anyone of the so-called financial pundits or high-paid analysts predicted the collapse of the financial system. Meanwhile, the disappointed public's distrust has assumed drastic proportions, and there's nothing left to do for the experts other than to confess their bewilderment. "We're groping in the dark," they say, or, "There's no theory that can predict exchange rates," and so on. No wonder that some shareholders prefer to trust their astrologers instead. Others leave it up to their cleaning lady.

The mood among the forecasters was not always quite so bleak. Since 1950 or thereabouts, many market economists began to believe that they could get a grip on the incalculable nature of the financial markets through the use of mathematical models. Their confidence soon turned into full-blown hubris. Those who tried to argue with words instead of equations were written off as dinosaurs. The classical economists simply couldn't compete with the formal elegance of abstract models that appeared to offer a new and wonderful precision. Naturally, these financial theories were based without exception on probability calculations, and blessing was given to them and the experts behind them in the guise of several Nobel Prizes.

Those working in the money markets didn't hesitate for very long before making use of the new instruments. The story of Long-Term Capital Management (LTCM), a hedge fund that was founded in 1994 and had securities worth $1.25 trillion on its books only four years later, offers an instructive example. With a relatively small capital of $4 billion the fund yielded a 30%–40% return in its first years, a result that makes the miracle of the loaves and fishes looks rather modest. Myron Scholes and Robert C. Merton served as managers of the fund and received the Nobel Prize for their singular achievements. The instruments they were using at the time were known only to a minority of specialists: asset-backed commercial papers (ABCPs), carry trades, collateralized debt obligations (CDOs), options, naked short selling, derivatives, and other even more exotic 'products'.

Just as with the atomic industry, Scholes and his comrades-in-arms reckoned the probability of a core meltdown to be negligible. Statistically speaking, the probability of the crash of 1987 actually occurring was only $1:10^{50}$—a risk that insiders regarded as small enough to be ignored. They would have been better off listening to the mathematicians, who recognized early on the weaknesses inherent in the risk models hedge fund managers and their competitors were relying on.

Already in 2004, long before the current financial crisis, Benoît Mandelbrot and Richard Hudson published a book that explains exactly why this was a mistake: In *The (Mis)Behavior of Markets: A Fractal View of Risk, Ruin, and Reward*, the authors suggest that current risk models are blind to the possibility of extreme occurrences because they are based on Gauß's notion of normal distribution: "This completely contradicts the reality of the market ... It's not the ordinary business days that decide whether one makes big profits or losses, but instead the days on which dramatic events occur." It all depends precisely on those values that are at the outer edges of the bell curve.

But there's yet another source of errors. As mathematician Yuri Manin has recently pointed out, the statistical models used by traders, banks, and insurance corporations are "to a considerable degree ... encoded in the software of their computers. These models thus become a hidden and highly influential part of the actions, our computerized 'collective unconscious'." To the extent that this software has come to be deemed indispensable, Manin recommends "risk management based upon models that use pessimistic 'Lévy distributions' rather than omnipresent Gaussians," which "paradoxically tends to flatten the shock waves and thus avoid major disasters." Mandelbrot and Hudson, meanwhile, rely on fractal models. However, neither of them expects these alternatives to offer a miracle cure. Mandelbrot even unpicked the Black-Scholes equations (their Nobel Prize endorsement notwithstanding). As would soon become evident, his warnings were to be proved right.

In 1998, due to 'unforeseen circumstances', LTCM found itself on the point of meltdown. The Federal Reserve and the International Monetary Fund feared a chain reaction that would lead to the collapse of the financial markets. A hasty rescue plan was drawn up. The names of the Samaritans rushing to lend a hand are known to every newspaper reader: Lehman Brothers, Merrill Lynch, Morgan Stanley, and Goldman Sachs. Deutsche Bank and Dresdner Bank were also along for the ride. The usual suspects, then, who were viewed at least in some quarters with mixed feelings.

Sympathy for the two Nobel Prize winners who forfeited their private capital in this debacle will doubtless have remained in check. If one or two onlookers enjoyed a certain momentary schadenfreude, that will also have been nipped in the bud. Merton is now back teaching economics at the Harvard Business School and training the analysts of the future, and Scholes, although convicted of tax evasion to the tune of $40 million, now heads up a new hedge fund and manages a portfolio of billions of dollars on behalf of his loyal clients.

Less than a decade after the downfall of LTCM the experts are once again surprised by a crisis in the financial markets that mirrors it in every detail except that this time the scale of the gambling has reached proportions that put the previous event in the shade. This chronic amnesia is clearly an integral part of the ahistorical nature of the theories that the financial world as a whole swears by.

X

Why is it that the majority of prognoses are self-evidently false? A first possible answer can be found in the basic principle underlying all classical probability calculation: the idea of normal distribution, which suggests a form of regularity whose extent has been fundamentally overestimated. If you think about it, the very proposition that reality obeys the model of normal distribution is rather odd. As every historical survey confirms, it's precisely not the frequent ordinary occurrences but the infrequent, extraordinary ones that deliver the most far-reaching consequences.

As an example of what's at stake, let's consider the question of meteorite collisions on earth. There are estimates as to how often this happens. Two American scientists, Clark Chapman and David Morrison, have been working on these calculations. They assure us that the probability of being killed by an asteroid is much greater than that of winning the lottery. But this is only valid for the tiniest pieces of rock. Projections based on the number of craters on the planet's surface and the frequency of asteroids and comets that pass close to the earth suggest that a crater on mainland, which would extinguish life, only comes to pass every two or three million years. The fact though that it might happen tomorrow afternoon rather mitigates their reassurances. To what extent their prognoses are actually correct must remain a matter of speculation, however, since after the event there will, in all probability, be no one left to savor the triumph of their theory.

In the logic of normal distribution exceptions to the rule serve only as troublesome disruptions. As a model, it appears helpless in the face of such 'gaffes' and always ends up looking ridiculous when applied to social processes. This might have to do with the fact that it originated in gambling, where each roll of the dice is unaffected by all those that have gone before for the simple reason that the roulette wheel has no memory. The opposite is true in history—something the majority of probability calculations do not seem to take into account. Thus, futurologists and market specialists, who continually present us with future event sequences and time lines on the basis of more or less sophisticated extrapolations at best, simply refuse to acknowledge the fact that any number of unforeseen events may render all their prognoses null and void.

A fairly trivial reflection will suffice to demonstrate the truth of this claim. No one doubts that people like Christ, Mozart, Hitler, or Stalin appear relatively infrequently on the world stage. In any frequency distribution they would appear as one of the outliers, where the bell curve is moving toward zero, just like the 8-foot-tall giant; and just like him, calculations would ignore them because of their extreme deviation from the norm. This would be a shame, of course, because then the prognosis would include neither the birth of Christianity and Classical music nor the advent of National Socialism and Stalinism. What this method obscures is the fact that in evolution, just as in history, catastrophes belong to the norm.

The forecasts also fail for another reason. Human beings have a number of characteristics that are absent in theory's favorite toy, the die, which possess neither herd instinct nor memory. Moreover, humans have the tendency to talk to each other, which makes everything even more complicated. Their interactions lead to an unpredictable number of feedbacks that make the tally of variables rise exponentially. Computational systems fail when faced with such tasks. Providing even rough numerical estimates for the reflexivity of economical and political systems would require levels of computational complexity beyond our capabilities. Take for instance an ordinary traffic jam. As soon as it is reported, drivers respond by seeking alternative routes, which become congested in turn as each frustrated driver reacts to what those ahead are doing. This creates a feedback loop in which individual elements can no longer be interpreted with any certainty. Thus we arrive at an inextricable interplay of self-fulfilling and self-refuting prophecies.

XI

It's difficult to boil down all the objections against the calculation of probability set out here to a single argument because they incorporate so many different points of departure. They are certainly too weak to knock the field off its pedestal. Fortunately for us, however, Italian philosopher Elena Esposito has demonstrated at a single stroke how it could be done in her 2008 book *The Fiction of Probable Reality*. Esposito cuts straight through the knot by proving that prognoses based on probability calculation are in effect nothing more than fictions. Future events don't occur with 9% or 99% probability; they either do or don't happen quite regardless of any predictions. That's why, she argues, it would be sheer chance (!) if any of the prophets were proved right, and we shouldn't be surprised that as a rule they simply wind up sabotaging themselves.

Esposito develops this persuasive thesis using arguments from systems theory and economics, the finer points of which need not be set out in detail here. Suffice it to paraphrase her conclusions. She casts doubts on the idea that probability theories bear any relation whatsoever to the historical world, and asserts instead that they are essentially self-referential, in the final analysis only serving the purposes of those who develop and apply them. Their illusory character resides precisely in the exactitude that the mathematical tool box merely *appears* to afford.

Esposito's reflections couldn't be more timely: She demonstrates that the currently dominant risk models rest on a tacitly accepted series of simplifications such as the dogma of market efficiency (the idea that markets always tend toward an equilibrium state), the notion that the players have access to complete information, and the assumption that they act rationally. Nobel laureate and mathematically-inclined theoretician Ronald H. Coase, too, hasn't minced his words on this subject: "Existing economics is a theoretical system which floats in the air and which bears little relation to what actually happens in the real world." Just like statistics and market research questionnaires, economic models function as a kind of alternative reality. The only ridiculous aspect of the situation resides in the fact that the inventors of these fictions keep getting them confused with reality and are not even aware of their confusion.

One question though Esposito wisely leaves open: Does her analysis also apply to descriptions of the subatomic sphere. If one can believe the physicists, they are the only ones living in a theoretical paradise without the prospect of ever being driven out by a skeptical angel. This Garden of Eden is the world of the quantum, in which there are only clouds of probability and no reality to speak of at all.

Certainly, Esposito is far too shrewd to dispute the continued right of probability theory to exist, thus eliminating her own subject, as it were. "A correctly calculated probability is still correct, even if it is not realized," she claims, "and perhaps it is useful for precisely this reason ... Its results are not true and they are not even meant to be." Fictions serve to make various modes of orientation possible that reality cannot provide. While reality has the exclusive monopoly on being singular, once and for all, the many fictive genres that culture invents are irrevocably pluralistic. Owing to their counterfactual nature they can show us what *would be possible if* ... The genre that Esposito chooses to compare probability theory with is the novel, and it would be foolish to dispute that novels have helped countless millions of readers to find their bearings in an improbable world.

XII

At this juncture, our thoughts turn back to the so-called real world and attempt to assume the perspective of the everyday, which generally has to deal with much more mundane concerns and much more trivial risks. The investor is constantly torn between fear and greed, herd instinct and risk aversion, with the result that his decisions are often completely irrational. In trying to secure his position against all possible dangers he comes up against a tragicomic paradox. For "the attempt to avoid risk," Esposito remarks, "is itself fraught with risk, and the need to seek security is in no way safe." Both of these needs naturally play into the hands of the insurance business and feed the ambitions of social policy makers.

At the same time, inside every timid conformist there is an adventurer trying to get out. For where risk has been eliminated boredom threatens. The judicious boss goes rough-terrain mountain biking on weekends, the apprentice at the savings bank relaxes with a spot of train surfing, the needlework teacher goes bungee jumping on the side, and the head teacher must cross the Sahara at all costs, where he will be intercepted by a gang of hostage takers. Now he, too, will have had his fifteen minutes of fame, appearing on TV after high-level politicians have brokered his release. The premium in the form of several million dollars of ransom money will fall in this case to the taxpayer.

But one doesn't need to consider extreme cases of this sort in order to see how little risk calculations inform our behavior. People who get married for love do not normally care very much that their chances of finding their 'soul mate' are rather low. The probability of meeting the 'one' among roughly a billion possible candidates is:

$$P(A) = \frac{\text{number of favorable outcomes for A}}{\text{number of possible outcomes}} = \frac{1}{1{,}000{,}000{,}000}$$

Of course, mathematicians have never been able to let this sleeping dog lie. Johannes Kepler had already carried out a detailed study of how one's chances of success in finding a mate could be increased. In a letter of 1613 to his patron, Baron Strahlendorf, he set out his method as follows: No fewer than twelve candidates must be examined. The solution he arrived at was, if truth be told, rather more intuitive than mathematically stringent. Even Gauß, who was all too familiar with the pitfalls of probability, wrote in resigned tones to his friend János Bolyai, a pioneer of non-Euclidian geometry: "Alas it is almost certain that marriage is a lottery, with many blanks and precious few winning tickets. May Heaven permit that if one day I play this game, I do not draw a blank." Once again, we discern the almost genetic relationship between theory and the desire to gamble.

It was not until the 20th century that a number of solutions for the dilemma of courtship were suggested that at last held water in theory. How can the chances of success be optimized in a rational way? This question is at the root of the so-called 'marriage problem', which is also known as the 'secretary' or 'best choice' problem. Let's assume there are n potential partners, where n can be any number. The sequence in which they are reviewed is random. After each interview the candidate is either rejected or accepted. The decision must be based solely on the candidate's place in the ranking so far: better or worse than the candidates reviewed up until then. On being rejected a candidate must withdraw. But when should one call a halt to the search? For this, there's a rule: If the number of candidates is big enough, it is recommended that one reject the first n/e candidates (where e is Euler's number 2.718 ...) and marry the next one who is better than all predecessors. This rule also applies if the number of candidates is one million. The odds of finding the best one by this method are $1/e$, which means roughly 37%. Not to be sniffed at, and significantly better than one in a billion!

"But still not good enough," says the person actually looking for a husband or wife. The 'one and only' could still be hidden in the other 63%. (Therein lies a possible cause for the high divorce rates.) Besides, this so-called 'stopping method' has the disadvantage of being cumbersome; and what's more, not every potential partner will necessarily be best pleased. Perhaps that's why those looking to be married generally remain convinced that they can make the one and only right choice without any algorithm.

XIII

Our happiness is a precarious business indeed. Pierre Basieux is certainly right in observing that the calculation of probability as a branch of mathematics is just as precise as geometry, algebra, and analysis. "One shouldn't confuse it, however," he cautions, "with the conclusions that can be drawn from applying probability models to the world in which we live. Just as it is impossible to prove an axiom, it is also impossible to prove that probabilities have any existence outside the purely mathematical realm."

Basieux is not the only one to arrive at this conclusion. In one of the dazzling formulations for which he is famous, systems theorist Niklas Luhmann speaks of the "paradox of the probability of the improbable." And even Aristotle already observed in *Poetics*: "It is probable that many a thing may happen contrary to probability."

It would appear, then, that science in its determined mission to drive fortune out of our lives has not enjoyed singular success. This could well be because we ourselves owe our existence to a long chain of extremely improbable events. In this way, our good fortune—along with our misfortunes—has managed to evade all the wonderful calculations we have dreamed up over the centuries. All that remains for us is the possibility, once in a while, of grasping Caerus by the forelock and seizing the right moment.

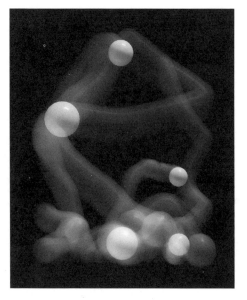

"There's a reason that one speaks of 'ghostly' appearances in the subatomic field, in the face of which common sense fails, just as when confronted with the trinity, the theodicy, or the question of free will in classical theology."
H. M. ENZENSBERGER

ON THE METAPHYSICAL ANTICS
OF
MATHEMATICS

Leibniz claims that mathematics is a form of consolation, that through mathematics one can be vouchsafed an inspiring insight into the divine order of being. The philosopher was not the only one to see in God the ultimate mathematician. One could almost think of him as a kabbalist. His project to create a *mathesis universalis* relied on the notion that in a series of logical steps mathematics can unlock secrets that are beyond ordinary human understanding.

Now, one doesn't need to know very much about the history of religion and mathematical thinking in order to realize that Leibniz's speculations were based on ideas that go back to pre-Classical times. For example, they can already be found in the ancient Indian Sulbasutras. Astronomy was probably the first abstract science. The birth of mathematics from the observation of the heavens was inextricably linked in all early civilizations to the birth of religious systems.

One might object that this interdependence is now primarily of archaeological interest. When all is said and done, modern science, at least from the Enlightenment on, can be thought of as the enterprise most securely immunized against all assaults from metaphysics. One has to go back a long way to find someone like Kepler, an astronomer with mystical tendencies, who discoursed on the harmony of the spheres and asserted: "The original archetype of all perfect geometric figures dwells in the spirit of the Creator; it is part of His eternity."

In fact, Kepler was drawing on a specifically European tradition going back at least to Plato, whose doctrine of ideas had served for centuries as the unchallenged foundation of mathematical thinking. The truth of mathematics, Plato held, lies beyond the empirical realm. The classical modern formulation of this thesis can be found in Descartes' Fifth Meditation, where the philosopher insists for instance that he didn't invent the characteristics of a triangle, which exist entirely independently of human observation. But Descartes didn't stop there: In the same Meditation, the father of the principle of doubt sets out to prove the existence of God and the eternal life of the soul. This goal was surely far from the mind of the number theorist Abraham Fraenkel. But he, too, asserts: "The mathematician does not *invent* the objects of his science—he *discovers* them." In other words, even if there were no mathematicians, the existence of mathematical objects wouldn't be altered in any way. If one follows this account the question of how one should conceive of the extramundane ontological status accorded to such mathematical objects remains open. Many of the modern disciples of Platonism have turned their backs on the religious roots of the doctrine. They prefer a leaner, more secular version. But it is noteworthy that from Isaac Newton to Alexander Grothendieck there have always been mathematicians who were no strangers to religious speculation. The Indian number theorist Srinivasa Ramanujan is reported as saying: "An equation for me has no meaning, unless it represents a thought of God."

Kurt Gödel, one of the greatest mathematicians of the 20th century, has even tried to use predicate logic in order to make the ontological argument for the proof of the existence of God formulated by Anselm of Canterbury in the 11th century completely watertight. (According to Oskar Morgenstern, one of the founders of game theory, Gödel did this not because he believed in God, but because he was persuaded by the logic of the argument. He called on "certain theological doctrines that have been preached for over 2000 years, albeit mixed with a good deal of nonsense. If one reads what has been asserted as dogma in the various churches over the course of time, and in some cases still is, it's quite astounding; for example, according to Catholic dogma the benevolent Lord has created the majority of human beings with the express purpose of condemning them to eternal damnation.")

It was also Gödel who made a decisive intervention in the foundational crisis in mathematics when formalists, constructivists, and the so-called intuitionists turned against the Platonist model in a bid to drive any metaphysical inclinations from the subject of mathematics once and for all. Simply put, these various, and in themselves diverging, approaches all understand mathematics as a purely human activity predicated on abstraction from experience. American mathematician Erret Bishop sets out the constructivist thesis as follows: "Mathematics belongs to man, not to God. We are not interested in properties of the positive integers that have no descriptive meaning for finite man. When a man proves a positive integer to exist, he should show how to find it. If God has mathematics of his own that needs to be done, let him do it himself."

Kurt Gödel, who, like Charles Hermite, Georg Cantor, Paul Bernays, Hermann Weyl, Godfrey Hardy, Roger Penrose, and many other modern mathematicians, had Platonist leanings, responded to the constructivists in one of his posthumously published manuscripts: "I am under the impression that after sufficient clarification of the concepts in question it will be possible to conduct these discussions with mathematical rigor, and that eventually … the Platonist view will be accepted as the only one tenable. I mean the view that mathematics describes a nonsensual reality that exists independently both of the acts and of the dispositions of the human mind, and is only perceived, and probably conceived very incompletely, by the human mind." "This view," Gödel ruefully adds, "is rather unpopular among mathematicians." This last comment was presumably aimed at Bertrand Russell, who had taken the easy way out by concluding from his encounters with Einstein, Wolfgang Pauli, and Gödel that "they all had a German bias towards metaphysics," as he famously wrote in his *Autobiography*.

For the hard-liners of the Vienna Circle gathered around Rudolf Carnap any proposition that exceeded the rigid rules of formal logic was tantamount to heresy. Like so many thinkers inspired by the Enlightenment before them, they, too, wanted to scotch any metaphysical speculations once and for all. Try as they might, they couldn't understand why not only Einstein and his colleagues but also billions of other people could still be thinking along lines that were roundly scorned in Bertrand Russell's seminars as so much outmoded superstition.

*

Another, quite different, yet in many ways related, philosophical question arises whenever mathematicians turn their attention to the fundamentals of their discipline. "How can it be," Einstein asked, "that mathematics, being after all a product of human thought which is independent of experience, is so admirably appropriate to the objects of reality?" Indeed, the methods and insights of mathematics

On the Metaphysical Antics of Mathematics

appear to be valid for the world we live in even though they were developed quite regardless of any possible application.

Any number of examples of these kinds of congruence can be given. When around 1800 Caspar Wessel and Carl Friedrich Gauß invented, or rather discovered, complex numbers, it hadn't occurred to them that they could be employed to solve problems in physics. It was only much later that they proved indispensible for the description of electromagnetic waves. Engineers use them every time they build a dynamo or a radio. Number theory developed its ideas about prime numbers long before it turned out that they were useful for encrypting confidential data. Even phenomena in the subatomic sphere that cannot be directly observed and that defy common sense can only be described with recourse to a mathematical theory developed over a hundred years before anyone had even imagined the existence of electrons. Without group theory, which built on the pioneering work of Évariste Galois, Niels Abel, Joseph Lagrange, Augustin Cauchy, Sophus Lie, and others, there would be no quantum mechanics. Richard Feynman's path integral, a precise reformulation of Erwin Schrödinger's wave equations, is unthinkable without complex numbers. And the symmetry of the gauge invariance depends on James Maxwell's differential equations of 1865, when quantum theory was not even imagined.

The following statement by Nicolas Bourbaki (the pseudonym for a collective of mathematicians who must be numbered among the formalists) reinforces this: "The big problem as regards the relationship between the empirical world and the mathematical world, namely, the close relationship between experimental phenomena and mathematical structures, appears to be confirmed in a highly unexpected way by the most recent discoveries in modern physics." "However," the statement continues with a certain resignation, "we don't know the reasons why this is the case."

In this, Bourbaki is correct; for it appears that none of the parties in the debate about the foundations of mathematics are in a position to solve the conundrum of the efficiency of mathematical ideas once and for all. This might well be the reason that so many mathematicians have turned their backs on the question, unimpressed by the philosophical discussions, which they evidently deem a waste of time. Others, again, concede that they are Platonists on Sundays and pragmatists during the working week. In general, this kind of attitude is characteristic of our civilization as a whole, which has for the most part remained unconvinced by metaphysical thinking.

Recently, there have been new initiatives coming from cognitive- and neuroscience, which have set out to find an answer to our conundrum. The argument runs like this: Since the human brain, as a product of evolution, is homologous with the universe that created it—albeit in a general rather than a specifically mathematical sense—any discovery or invention it makes must in principle always bear a structural relation to this universe, even if the discoveries themselves remain incomplete due to the brain's limited capacity. Of course, this proposition is good news for science. Since the world is incontrovertibly richer and more varied than the human brain, the latter has an inexhaustible task before it for as long as the species exists.

It has been suggested here and there that research will eventually succeed in finding conclusive answers to its basic questions. Its heroic age is over, the story goes, all it has to do now is fill one or two gaps, or else be at the service of technology. This kind of prognosis is mistaken, however, for the simple reason that compared to what exists all around us, our thinking is fundamentally underdeveloped. This can be seen well enough in the field of quantum mechanics, where, despite the fact that we can describe phenomena mathematically, our imaginations fall at the first hurdle when we try to comprehend them. Thus, in response to David Hilbert's famous words (from his 1930 Königsberg address): "For us, there is no *We don't know* ... We must know! We will know!," one will have to say: "Yes, but not quite ..."

And so it looks as if metaphysical thinking will never be driven out of mathematics completely. It seems to haunt the discussions at a subterranean level. There's a reason that one speaks of 'ghostly' appearances in the subatomic field, in the face of which common sense fails, just as when confronted with the trinity, the theodicy, or the question of free will in classical theology.

Rolf Landua is a physicist at the European Organization for Nuclear Research (CERN) and leads the ATHENA experiment to produce antihydrogen. On the naive, but unavoidable, question regarding the object of his research, he comments: "It might sound strange in the Mecca of particle physics, but none of us physicists knows what an elementary particle actually is. We can record its measurable characteristics (mass, electric charge, spin, etc.) with absolute precision; but what it actually is remains a mystery. People have gotten used to thinking of electrons as points without any physical dimensions. But this also leads to contradictions because mathematical models always have difficulties dealing with objects with a dimension of zero. One always ends up with infinity when one has to divide by zero." He then goes even further, asking himself whether God might have had a hand in the Big Bang—an idea that, he believes, cannot be straightforwardly refuted.

.*

A poet may possibly be permitted to offer, if not an explanation for the persistence of such questions, then at least a logical scheme. It might look like this:

1. There are problems

2. There are two kinds of problem.

2.1. There are solvable and insolvable problems.

2.1.1 There are two kinds of solvable problem.

2.1.1.1. There are solvable problems where it can be proved that they are solvable.

2.1.1.2. There are solvable problems where it cannot be proved that they are solvable.

2.1.2. There are two kinds of insolvable problem.

2.1.2.1. There are insolvable problems where it cannot be proved that they are insolvable.

2.1.2.2. There are insolvable problems where it can be proved that they are insolvable.

3. These are the problems that human beings have tried to solve since time immemorial.

But what has a classification like this got to do with mathematics? After all, Alfred Tarski, drawing on Gödel, was able to prove that the notion of truth cannot formally be defined; for every definition based on innumerable rules there is always one exception that demonstrates its own untruth. As American logician Alonso Church showed in 1936, in principle there is no reliable procedure for establishing whether any proposition can be proved or not.

In mathematics, the idea of basic plausibility still goes a long way, just as it does in theology. There is no shortage of examples. Are there infinitely many twin primes? The French mathematician Alphonse de Polignac formulated this conjecture over 150 years ago, and now it has been checked—at least to a value of $2{,}003{,}663{,}613 \times 2^{195{,}000}$. That's a number with approximately 59,000 zeros.[*] Common sense tells us that this should be enough. But no! A number theorist like Franz Mertens would never have been content with such a statement. Mertens' fame rests on a conjecture with which generations of scholars have wrestled. It has to do with Bernhard Riemann's legendary hypothesis of 1859 concerning the distribution of prime numbers, which was viewed as *the* unresolved mathematical problem of the century. In the hope of getting closer to a solution, Mertens developed an equation relating to Riemann's zeta function, or, to be more precise, to the zeros in it. He conjectured that his equation would work for any given value. (I'm perfectly willing to confess that I've only ever understood his conjecture when explained by a patient expert, but then, the very next day, I've always been incapable of reconstructing it. Luckily, that's not the issue here). Number theorists have taken infinite pains to prove the Mertens conjecture. For if it could be done, the validity of Riemann's hypothesis would follow. The conjecture has been tested numerically for the first few billion cases (up to $n = 10^{14}$), and it has worked every time. But this procedure doesn't yet amount to a proof. And in fact, in 1985 Herman te Riele and Andrew Odlyzko successfully refuted it, although they couldn't find any counterexamples. There has to be at least one though somewhere before the upper limit of 10^{156}, which is so ridiculously high that there's no chance of ever finding it. Why should this case be of interest? Because it demonstrates the inscrutable mysteries of the world of numbers. The problem Riemann identified is still

[*]On August 6, 2009, it was announced that a new record twin prime had been found: $65{,}516{,}468{,}355 \times 2^{333333} \pm 1$. (*Translator's Note*)

considered one of the great unsolved puzzles of modern mathematics.

The same is true of the celebrated Goldbach conjecture dating back to 1742, which has been verified for all values up to 10^{18}; but, like the doctrine of the immaculate conception, it has neither been proved nor refuted.

The tireless efforts of number theorists to remedy the situation are not entirely free of aspects of obsession. That's why the German mathematician Leopold Kronecker compared them to Homer's lotus eaters. It's not quite clear whether Kronecker remembered that in the *Odyssey* the lotus flower works like a drug, and that whoever falls prey to its intoxication forgets where he came from and where he is going, believing himself in paradise. As one can see, the high-altitude euphoria induced by this kind of mathematical thinking has certain metaphysical idiosyncrasies of its own that have little to do with reason.

*

This is nowhere more clearly demonstrated than when the concept of the infinite is invoked. As the history of mathematics makes plain, no good can come of having truck with the infinite. For thousands of years debates about the infinite had been the province of philosophy or theology, and for both disciplines the infinite had been highly suspect. The Pythagoreans saw it as a negative and destructive force and sought salvation in natural numbers. The Stoics proclaimed that even God couldn't grasp the infinite. And Augustine found it necessary to dedicate an entire chapter of *The City of God* to refuting this theory, which he considered blasphemous. "That numbers are infinite," he wrote "is certainly true. Does God therefore not know all of them? Does His knowledge extend only to a certain point in numbers while of the rest he is ignorant? Who is so lost to sense as to claim such a thing? Does not the Prophet say, 'Who brings out the host by number?' And the Savior says in the Gospels, 'The very hairs of your head are all numbered'. The infinity of numbers is not incomprehensible by him whose wisdom is infinite."

Mathematicians have also never been comfortable dealing with infinite values since they always lead to paradoxes and contradictions. Descartes tried to put an end to the difficulties by summarily declaring: "We won't wear ourselves out with disagreements about the infinite. Given that we are finite it would be a waste of time." Even the great Carl Friedrich Gauß protested against the use of infinite values and understood talk of them to be simply a *façon de parler*.

That's how things stood until Georg Cantor appeared on the scene with a brilliant idea. His concept of uncountable real numbers threw previous arguments into disarray. He demonstrated in the 1870s that there is an infinite hierarchy of infinities. His teacher and former mentor Leopold Kronecker—the same Kronecker who regarded number theorists as lotus eaters—couldn't come to terms with this idea. He accused Cantor of being a "corruptor of youth." "God (!) made the integers," he declared, "all else is the work of man." He insisted that mathematical deductions must make it possible to construct a mathematical conclusion in a finite number of steps. In this sense, he can be considered a forerunner of constructivism.

A nasty academic dispute ensued. Kronecker saw to it that Cantor was not appointed to a Chair either in Göttingen or Berlin, and even attempted, unsuccessfully, to prevent the publication of Cantor's findings. Cantor believed that the existence of transfinite numbers had been communicated to him by God. He had not, he claimed, invented them; he was simply the mouthpiece of the Lord, entrusted with communicating these ideas to humanity. This divine revelation drove him to abandon his mathematical work in 1885 and focus on theology. He became embroiled in an extended debate with leading Neo-Thomist thinkers and attempted to persuade them that his work had provided Christian philosophy with the first cogent proof of the infinite. The fact that Cantor, like Gödel after him, was plagued by recurring bouts of manic depression is perhaps not entirely a matter of chance. Other mathematicians who have grappled with infinitesimal values have guarded themselves against the risks with the kind of meticulous care that such encounters with the infinite demand.

More recently, a new attitude has become widespread, especially in IT and experimental mathematics, which is oriented purely towards praxis and prefers to leave insolvable problems well alone. Nuts that can't be cracked are best left to the theologians. That said, there are already signs that as a race we are simply too curious to make do with this kind of self-imposed limit for very long.

*

All speculation aside, one thing is certain: the abstractions of pure mathematics intervene in ways that are unforeseeable, yet precise and experimentally verifiable, when it comes to investigating and manipulating our environment. This undeniable efficiency has enormous consequences for our civilization, as Robert Musil pointed out over a century ago. "One might argue," Musil wrote in 1913, "that we live almost entirely from the results of mathematics, although they themselves have become a matter of indifference to mathematics. Thanks to mathematics we bake our bread, build our houses, and drive our vehicles. With the exception of a few handmade pieces of furniture, clothing, shoes, and children, everything comes to us through the intervention of mathematical calculations. All the life that whirls around us, runs, pauses is not only dependent on mathematics for its comprehensibility, but has effectively come into being through it ..." Most people never suspect to what degree their everyday life, but also their entire world picture, is dependent on the achievements of a long line of scientists whose names they have never heard.

"And suddenly," Musil continues, "when everything had been brought into the most beautiful kind of existence, the mathematicians—the ones who brood entirely within themselves—came upon something wrong in the fundamentals of the whole thing that absolutely could not be put right. They actually looked all the way to the bottom and found that the whole building was standing in midair." Long before Gödel, Musil had seen the writing on the wall and responded with equal degrees of pragmatic consolation and metaphysical hopelessness: "But the machines worked! We must assume from this that our existence is a pale ghost; we live it, but actually only on the basis of an error, without which it would not have arisen. Today there is no other possibility of having such fantastic visionary feelings as mathematicians do."

"Moreover, humans have the tendency to talk to each other, which makes everything even more complicated. Their interactions lead to an unpredictable number of feed-backs that make the tally of variables rise exponentially."
H. M. ENZENSBERGER

SELECT BIBLIOGRAPHY

Pierre Basieux, *The Adventure of Mathematics: Bridges Between Reality and Fiction [Abenteuer Mathematik: Brücken zwischen Wirklichkeit und Fiktion]* (1999).

Erret Bishop, *Foundations of Constructive Analysis* (1967).

Nicolas Bourbaki, cited in Pierre Basieux.

Ronald H. Coase, "Interview with Ronald Coase," Inaugural Conference of the International Society for New Institutional Economics, St. Louis, USA (September 17, 1997).

Albert Einstein, *Sidelights on Relativity* (1922), translated by G. B. Geoffrey and W. Perret (2010).

Elena Esposito, *The Fiction of Probable Reality [Probabilità improbabili. La realtà della finzione nella società moderna]* (2008).

Kurt Gödel, *Unpublished Essays and Lectures*, vol. 3 of *Collected Works*, 5 vols., edited by Solomon Feferman (1986–2003).

Leopold Kronecker, cited in: Eric Temple Bell, *Men of Mathematics* (1986).

Rolf Landua, *On the Edge of the Dimensions [Am Rand der Dimensionen]* (2008).

Niklas Luhmann, *The Society of Society [Die Gesellschaft der Gesellschaft]* (1997).

Benoît Mandelbrot and Richard L. Hudson, *The (Mis)Behavior of Markets: A Fractal View of Risk, Ruin, and Reward* (2004).

Yuri I. Manin, "Truth as Value and Duty: Lessons of Mathematics," International Symposium of the Balzan Foundation on "Truth in the Humanities, Science and Religion" (Lugano, Switzerland, May 16–17, 2008).

Odo Marquard, *In Defense of the Accidental,* translated by Robert M. Wallace (1991).

Oskar Morgenstern, cited in Kurt Gödel.

Robert Musil, "The Mathematical Man" (1913), in: *Precision and Soul: Essays and Addresses*, edited and translated by David S. Luft and Burton Pike (1995).

Ian Stewart, *Does God play Dice? The Mathematics of Chaos* (1989).

Poet and essayist **HANS MAGNUS ENZENSBERGER** has been at the forefront of the German and European cultural scenes for more than four decades. He has published over sixty books of poetry, prose, and cultural and political commentary that have been translated into more than forty languages. The many honors and awards he has received include The Georg Büchner Prize, the Heinrich Böll Prize, the Heinrich Heine Prize, the Erich Maria Remarque Peace Prize, and the Griffin Lifetime Recognition Award.

Award-winning author and translator of German poetry and prose **KAREN LEEDER** is Professor of Modern German Literature at the University of Oxford and a Fellow of New College, Oxford, England.

Internationally acclaimed artist **DAVID FRIED** was a key player, alongside Keith Haring and Richard Hambleton, in pioneering the New York street-art scene of the early 1980s. In 1989, Fried moved his studio to Germany in pursuit of Europe's socio-cultural complexity as an inspirational backdrop for his increasingly scientific and philosophic brand of art. There his fascination with specifically human relationships led to deeper insights into dynamic relationships in general, which soon crystallized as the conceptual core for all his forthcoming artistic endeavors, including the ongoing series of sound-stimulated interactive kinetic sculptures titled 'self-organizing still life'. All images created for this book are based on such self-organizing still lifes activated by Hans Magnus Enzensberger's words read aloud.

GERD GIGERENZER is Director of the Center for Adaptive Behavior and Cognition at the Max Planck Institute for Human Development in Berlin, Germany, and author of the internationally acclaimed *Gut Feelings: The Intelligence of the Unconscious.*